HOW

Financial
statements

A detailed guide to increasing knowledge of investment opportunities through understanding financial statements.

Canadian Cataloguing in Publication Data

Main entry under title:

How to read financial statements

Issued also in French under title: Comment lire les etats financiers.

Rev. ed. Includes index. ISBN 1-894289-57-9

1. Financial statements. I. Canadian Securities Institute

HF5681.B2C348 2000   657'.3   C00-930755-9

First Printing 1971 by the Canadian Securities Institute

Revised and Reprinted 1973, 1980, 1982, 1983, 1984, 1985, 1987, 1988, 1989, 1990, 1992, 1994, 1995, 1998, 2000

Copyright 2000, by the Canadian Securities Institute   *Printed and bound in Canada*

HOW TO READ Financial statements

Published by the Canadian Securities Institute (CSI) and distributed by the Investor Learning Centre of Canada (ILC).

The CSI is the national educational organization for Canada's securities industry and an internationally recognized authority in investment education.

The ILC is an independent non-profit organization dedicated to helping Canadians take charge of their financial futures through impartial educational materials.

About this book

Each year, tens of thousands of companies in North America produce glossy 50-odd-page publications called annual reports. These are perhaps the most important tools for people like us. They provide a depth of information about a company which you would be hard-pressed to find elsewhere. What's more, annual reports are free and much of the information in them is presented in an interesting and understandable way.

Of course, some parts of the annual report are purely promotional. Companies will often spend thousands of dollars hiring marketing experts to write promotional material for their annual reports. In fact, when all is said and done, perhaps the most important information in the annual report can be found in four rather drab pages somewhere in the middle of the report. These are the financial statements.

To a novice, financial statements might look like columns of meaningless numbers. In reality, though, financial statements are like a scorecard on a company's operations. They show you what a company owns and what it owes, as well as how profitable – or unprofitable – it has been. If you're thinking about investing in a company's stocks or bonds, then it's important for you to be able to understand and analyze these statements. They can reveal much about a company's financial health.

This book aims to give you the know-how — and the fortitude — to scour through an annual report like a pro. The first section takes you step-by-step through the four main types of financial statements. It explains each of the many items you will find in each statement. When you understand what each item in the financial statements represents, you will better be able to grasp how most businesses work. That's the other thing about financial statements — they're a window on the world of how businesses operate. You'll be amazed how much you can learn about how businesses are run when you can read financial statements.

The second section of this book shows you how you can gain even more insight into a company by probing the relationships between two or more numbers in the financial statements. For instance, by dividing the company's profits by the number of shares investors own, you will learn how to calculate how much profit the company earned for each share. This is known as the Earnings Per Share (EPS) calculation, and you'll be learning about it and many other ratios as you work your way through the book.

Which raises an important point – how you should go about reading this book. We suggest you read it twice. The first time should be to get a general sense of what it covers. The second reading should be more methodical and focussed. A good idea on the second reading is to have a few annual reports handy so that you can cross reference information in this book to real-life financial statements.

For your convenience, we've included sample financial statements for Trans-Canada Retail Stores Ltd., a fictitious retail chain. You'll find them at the back of the book. We refer to them in the descriptions of the different items found in the financial statements — and also in the calculations in part two.

Because we wanted to make things as easy as possible for you, our sample financial statements differ from real financial statements in the following ways:

• Previous years' figures are not shown

• There are no notes to financial statements

• The consecutive numbers on the left hand side of the statements, which are used in explaining ratio calculations, don't appear in real reports.

Although the sample financial statements will help you, we strongly recommend you get hold of a few real annual reports. These are easy to get if you call a public company's investor relations department. You can also order free annual reports through special services advertised in the stock tables in newspapers like the Globe and Mail's Report on Business.

The reason you should make yourself familiar with annual reports from actual companies is that different companies use different terms to describe items in their statements. The sooner you become comfortable with the various terms used, the quicker your learning will be and the more confident you will become. If there's an item in an annual report you don't understand, call the company's investor relations department and ask for an explanation. No one, not even experienced professionals, can be expected to know all the different terms and meanings accountants use in financial statements.

Also, when you compare annual reports from different companies you will find varying amounts of information. This is because some companies disclose more information than others. Generally, the more information provided, the better you will be able to analyze the company.

Besides providing financial statements, annual reports also contain other valuable information, such as the president's (or directors') report to shareholders –which covers highlights of the past year, comments on the outlook for the current year, and discussion of such items as labor relations, expansion plans, management and product changes.

The report may also include comparative statistics for the last five or ten years, information on different segments of the company's business, a simplified summary of the financial statements for shareholders, graphs, charts and pictures of the company's plants, products and services.

A more recent, and valuable, addition to the annual report is a section called Management's Discussion and Analysis (MD&A). It normally precedes the financial statements and is supposed to put the company's results into context. You'll find that the information in the "outlook" section of the MD&A is very helpful in understanding what company management believes the major issues are facing the company. However, the level of detail in the MD&A varies by company, so you often have to do your own analysis. Which, of course, is something you should do anyway.

So, without further ado let's plunge into the first part of our exploration: understanding the four financial statements you will find in all annual reports. These are the balance sheet, the earnings statement, a statement of retained earnings (sometimes presented as a combined statement of earnings and retained earnings) and a statement of changes in financial position.

Part 1

THE BALANCE SHEET

The balance sheet shows you a company's financial position on a specific date. In annual reports, that date is the last day of the company's fiscal year. While many companies have a fiscal year ending Dec. 31, this is not always the case. Many broadcasting and media companies have an Aug. 31 fiscal year end, while banks and trust companies traditionally end their fiscal year on Oct. 31.

One side of the balance sheet — often the left side — shows you what the company owns and what is owing to it. These items are called assets. The other side of the balance sheet shows (1) what the company owes, called liabilities, and (2) the company's shareholders' equity or net worth, which represents the shareholders' interest in the company. Shareholders' equity is the excess of the company's assets over its liabilities. So the company's total assets are equal to the sum of the company's liabilities, plus the shareholders' equity.

Using the Trans-Canada Retail Stores Ltd. financial statements at the back of the book, the relationship between items on the balance sheet is as follows:

Simple Balance Sheet

Assets.................................$19,761,000		Liabilities..............................$ 6,402,000	
		Shareholders' Equity..........$13,359,000	
		Total Liabilities and	
Total Assets.......................$19,761,000		Shareholders' Equity..........$19,761,000	

The above equation between balance sheet items may alternatively be expressed as:

Assets...$19,761,000	
Less: Liabilities..$ 6,402,000	
Equals: Shareholders' Equity...$13,359,000	

Shareholders' equity is often called the company's book value. However, this item does not always indicate how much shareholders will get for their ownership interest in a sale. The market value of the shareholders' interest may be worth a lot more or less than book value, largely depending on the company's earning power and prospects.

The Six Kinds of Assets

Taking each class of asset one by one and in the order in which they are shown in the Trans-Canada Retail balance sheet, we will see what they are and what they tell us about the company.

1. Current Assets (items 1 to 5 on the sample financial statements p 16-20)

Current Assets are cash and assets that can be turned into cash immediately or which, in the normal course of business, will be turned into cash within one year. Current assets are the most important group of assets. They determine a firm's ability to pay its daily operating expenses. On the balance sheet, current assets are usually listed in order of liquidity. Those that can be converted into cash quickest are listed first.

Current assets can be divided into five broad groups:

• *Cash* on hand or in the bank

• *Marketable securities* – bonds and stocks that can be easily sold for cash

• *Receivables* - money owing to the company for goods or services it has sold. Because some customers don't pay their bills, an item called allowance for doubtful accounts is often subtracted from

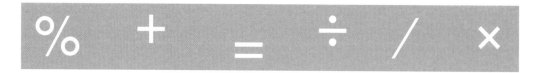

receivables. This is management's estimate of the amount that won't be collected. The amount mostly isn't shown separately on the balance sheet because it's assumed adequate allowance has been made.

• *Inventories* – the goods and supplies a company keeps in stock. A furniture manufacturer that sells chairs to Trans-Canada Retail will have inventories of raw materials like fabric and wood, work-in-progress like assembled chair frames and completed chairs ready for shipping.

Inventories are changed by successive steps into cash. Raw materials are processed into finished goods. Finished goods are sold on 30, 60 or 90 days or longer credit terms and give rise to receivables. These receivables become due and are paid off in cash. This process goes on day after day, giving the company money to pay for wages, raw materials, taxes and other expenses, and ultimately to make profits from which dividends may be paid to shareholders.

Inventories are valued at original cost or current market value – whichever is lower.

There are three commonly used methods of determining the cost of inventories:

• Average cost of all items in inventory

• FIFO (first-in-first-out) – items acquired earliest are assumed to be used or sold first (most commonly used method in Canada)

• LIFO (last-in-first-out) – items acquired most recently are assumed to be used or sold first (acceptable for accounting but not for income tax purposes in Canada)

If prices are changing, each of these methods produces a different inventory value – and therefore a different profit. When prices are rising, the FIFO method gives the higher inventory and higher profit figure, and the LIFO method will produce the lower inventory and lower profit.

• *Prepaid expenses* – payment made by the company for services to be received in the near future. They are the equivalent of cash since they eliminate the need to pay cash for goods or services in the immediate future. Rents, insurance premiums and taxes, for example, are sometimes paid in advance. For accounting purposes, their cost is generally spread over the periods when the company benefits from this expenditure.

2. Miscellaneous Assets (item 7)

Miscellaneous Assets are assets that are neither current nor fixed. The most common are:

• Cash surrender value of life insurance

• Amounts due from directors, officers and employees of the company

• Investments of a long-term nature, e.g. investment in, or money lent, to a supplier

• Investments in, and advances to, subsidiary and affiliated companies

3. Fixed Assets (item 8)

Fixed Assets are land, buildings, machinery, tools and equipment of all kinds, trucks, furnishings and so on, used in the day-to-day operations of a business. Unlike current assets, which are converted by successive steps into cash, the value of fixed assets to a company lies in their use in producing goods and services for sale, rather than in their sale value. They are not intended to be sold.

A company's proportion of fixed assets to total assets depends on the type of business. Fixed assets of a public utility, railway or pulp and paper company form a very large part of total assets; those of an insurance or finance company may be a relatively small proportion of total assets.

Fixed assets are shown on the balance sheet at original cost, including installation and other acquisition expenses. Except for land, fixed assets are depreciated each year and the total accumulated depreciation is deducted from the original cost. The value of fixed assets recorded on the balance sheet after deducting depreciation is called the assets' net book value. If a fixed asset is sold, its original cost and related depreciation are removed from the balance sheet. The difference between the fixed asset's sale price and that asset's net book value is a profit (or loss) which is treated as non-operating income (or expense).

Depreciation

Depreciation: Fixed assets - other than land - wear out in time or otherwise lose their usefulness. Between the time an asset is acquired and when it's no longer economically useful, its value decreases. This loss in value over several years is called depreciation. Depletion is a similar term applied to resource assets, and amortization is a term used to describe the writing-off of intangible assets.

To spread the cost of fixed assets over their useful years, companies record depreciation expense against each year's earnings. This is done because fixed assets are used to produce goods or services and depreciation is, therefore, a cost of doing business just like wages and other operating expenses.

Depreciation is the ordinary process where plant and equipment wear out. The amount recorded as depreciation each year is based on each asset's original cost, its expected life, and the probable salvage or scrap value, if any, when it is withdrawn from service.

There are several ways these amounts can be assigned to each accounting period. Most public companies in Canada use the straight line method, where an equal amount is charged to each period. The declining balance method is also often used. It applies a fixed percentage (usually double the straight line rate), rather than a fixed dollar amount, to the outstanding balance to determine the expense to be charged in each period. This amount is deducted from the fixed asset balance to determine the amount against which the percentage will be applied in the next period - thus the term declining balance. This method is used frequently by smaller companies, as it usually agrees with the method of computing "capital cost allowance" for income tax purposes. There are other less common methods.

The example in Table 1 on page 14 shows the calculation of depreciation by the straight line and declining balance methods.

Depreciation is intended to assign the cost (net of salvage value) for fixed assets over their useful lives. And it gives a realistic matching of earnings to expenses in a fiscal period so a company's net income can be determined. One common misconception about accumulated depreciation is that it represents actual cash in a bank account. It does not. Yes, the annual depreciation charge prevents the distribution of this amount of earnings to shareholders, but these retained earnings don't remain idle. They may be used by the company in any way it sees fit – to buy inventory, securities, new fixed assets, meet sinking fund payments on debt issues, or pay other obligations.

It is impossible to actually trace the final use of any given dollar coming into a company. The earnings statement shows that a certain amount of cash comes into a company each year from the sale of its products and that a certain amount is spent for operating expenses and income taxes. What is left over represents an inflow of cash available to the company to buy assets, repay debt, pay dividends and use for other purposes. The net income may be less than this net inflow of cash because depreciation (a non-cash expense) has been deducted to arrive at net income for the year.

Depletion

Depletion: is similar to depreciation and is usually used by mining, oil, natural gas and timber companies, and other extractive industries. The assets of these industries are natural wealth such as minerals in the ground or standing timber. As these assets are developed and sold, the company loses part of its assets with each sale. These are known as wasting assets and the decrease in value is referred to as depletion. An allowance for depletion is made, recognizing that

Table 1

Methods of Calculating Depreciation

Suppose a piece of equipment bought by XYZ Co, Ltd. at $100,000 is expected to have a useful life of eight years and a salvage value of $10,000. The annual depreciation for this asset utilizing the straight line method is:

$$\frac{\$1000,000 - \$10,0000}{8} \quad = \quad \$11,250$$

and the depreciation rate is 12.5% (100%/8) per year for each of the eight years of expected usefulness.

The depreciation rate under the declining balance method would be 25% (double the straight line rate of 12.5%) on each year's remaining balance. Thus, in Year 1: $100.000 depreciated at 25% = $25,000. In Year 2: $75,000 ($100,000 - $25,000) depreciated at 25% = $18,750. By the end of eight years, using the declining balance method of calculating depreciation, there is an undepreciated balance of $10,011 as the following table shows:

Depreciation: Straight Line versus Declining Balance
Cost of Assets: $100,000 Salvage Value: $10,000 Useful Life: 8 Years

| Fiscal Year-End | Straight Line | | Declining Balance | |
	Depreciation Charge	Book Value on Balance Sheet	Depreciation Charge	Book Value on Balance Sheet
1st	$11,250	$88,750	$25,000	$75,000
2nd	$11,250	$77,500	$18,750	$56,250
3rd	$11,250	$66,250	$14,063	$42,188
4th	$11,250	$55,000	$10,547	$31,641
5th	$11,250	$43,750	$ 7,910	$23,730
6th	$11,250	$32,500	$ 5,933	$17,798
7th	$11,250	$21,250	$ 4,449	$13,348
8th	$11,250	$10,000	$ 3,337	$10,011

as companies sell their natural assets, they must recover not only the cost of extraction, but also the original cost of acquiring such natural resources before a profit can be made.

Annual allowances for depreciation and depletion appear as non-cash charges against earnings in the earnings statement. They not only reflect the using-up of assets, but also properly match expenses with related income. So it is possible for a company to add considerably to its cash resources for the year, yet show little or no net earnings, if substantial depreciation charges were made. These effects will be reflected in the statement of changes in financial position, where the cash from operations is reported.

The accumulated allowances for depreciation and depletion usually appear on the asset side of the balance sheet as a direct deduction from the fixed assets they apply to. One figure for accumulated depreciation is usually shown for all assets. The breakdown of depreciation by each fixed asset class is relegated to the notes to the financial statements.

4. Capitalized Leases and Interest

Capitalizing refers to the recording of an expenditure as an asset rather than as an expense. This is done to allow for the spreading of an expense over more than one accounting period. Two of the most common types of capitalized items are leases and interest.

Capitalized Leases: Normally, only assets which are legally owned by a company are recorded as fixed assets in its financial statements. Certain leases, however, are considered to be merely another means of financing the acquisition of an asset. In these cases, the lessee carries substantially all the risks and benefits that come with property ownership. So this type of lease (referred to as capitalized leases) is recorded as if the lessee had actually bought the asset and assumed a liability.

The item (e.g. building, equipment, etc.) that's leased is shown on

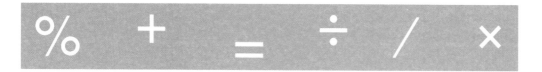

the asset side of the balance sheet, recorded at its fair market value, and treated like any other fixed asset that the company "owns."

Similarly, the amount owed (e.g. capital lease) to acquire the asset is shown on the liability side of the balance sheet and recorded as the present value of future lease payments. This obligation is treated like a long-term debt.

Capitalized Interest: Some companies, such as oil and gas companies active in exploration, capitalize much of their interest costs instead of expensing them when incurred. The argument for doing this? No revenue is generated during the exploration phase, and deferring this interest cost to a later date gives a better matching of revenues and expenses. This argument has some merit, but capitalizing interest could be used artificially to smooth out income during periods when earnings are actually quite volatile. As with other accounting policies, once adopted, the policy should not be changed unless warranted by unusual circumstances. This practice will reduce the potential for abuse.

The practice of capitalizing interest is also followed by utilities during periods of construction. The interest cost is added to the cost of the assets constructed, and affects the base used to calculate utility rates charged to customers.

Interest capitalized is not always added to the cost of the related asset. Sometimes it is recorded as a deferred charge (discussed next). The amount capitalized is shown as an asset on the balance sheet and reduced in subsequent periods as amounts are recorded as expenses.

5. Deferred Charges (item 9)

Deferred Charges is another type of asset often shown on the balance sheet. These charges represent payments made by the company for which the benefit will extend to the company over many years. So it's similar to prepaid expenses (described earlier) except that the benefits received extend for a longer period. The cost of such items, for accounting purposes, is spread over several years by annual write-offs. This gradual writing-off of deferred charges and intangible assets – described next – is called amortization, and is the equivalent of depreciation of fixed assets. At the date of the balance sheet, the balance of amounts paid for benefits which have not been totally used is shown as an asset. Deferred charges may represent expenses from issuing bonds, commission paid on the sale of capital stock, organizational expenses or research expenses.

6. Intangible Assets (item 10)

Intangible Assets are assets which cannot be touched, weighed or measured. They aren't available for paying a going business's debts. They usually have little value if the company goes out of business. Common examples are goodwill, patents, copyrights, franchises and trademarks. Intangible assets, which may be grouped on the balance sheet under the headings "miscellaneous assets" or "other assets," are valuable legal rights essential to the operations of the company.

The realizable value in cash of intangible assets is uncertain. So most companies show them on the balance sheet at a low value. This accounting practice indicates that management is being quite conservative because the intangible assets listed may be quite valuable to the company.

Goodwill deserves special mention. It's often defined as the probability that a regular customer will continue to return to do business. If people get into the habit of doing business with a firm because of its location or reputation for fair dealing and good products, they will probably continue that habit, at least to some extent, even though the firm changes hands.

The buyer of a business is often willing to pay for its "good name" in addition to the value of its assets. Goodwill may also signify the

amount that a purchaser of a company will pay for the good management of the company. It will appear on consolidated (or combined) balance sheets as that amount paid for the shares over their net asset value.

The values given to intangible assets on the balance sheet should be viewed cautiously. If these assets have any real value at all, it's due more to their contribution to earning power than to their saleability as an asset. A trademark may mean much to a company from the point of view of sales, for example, yet, in itself, it might not have any sale value as an asset.

Six Types of Liabilities

Now we'll turn our attention to the other side of the balance sheet, and examine each class of liability and shareholders– equity.

1. Current Liabilities (items 12 to 16)

Current liabilities are debts incurred by a company in the ordinary course of its business, which have to be paid within a short time – a year at the most. The Trans-Canada Retail balance sheet shows five common types of current liabilities:

• *Bank advances* are its short-term loans from financial institutions

• *Accounts payable* include unpaid bills for raw materials and supplies

• *Dividends payable* are funds that have been set aside after the company declares a dividend

• *Income taxes payable* are taxes to be paid to the government in the near term

• *First mortgage bonds due within one year* are the current portion of the company's long-term debt

All other kinds of obligations which must be met within a year are also included in current liabilities. Some of these are outstanding wages and salaries, bank and bond interest, legal fees, pension payments, and property and excise taxes. In every case, the liability is a very definite one which has to be met. Quite often, the values given to assets may shrink, but liabilities, particularly current ones, never do.

2. Deferred Income Taxes (item 18)

Public companies must report to their shareholders through financial statements and to appropriate levels of government through their tax returns. Deferred tax results when tax shown on a company's income statement is different from tax reported in its income tax return. This difference happens because tax on income statements is calculated according to strict Canadian Institute of Chartered Accountants (CICA) guidelines, and tax paid is based on tax returns filed under federal and provincial Income Tax Acts and regulations. Deferred tax is the difference between taxes paid (which are based on the tax form) and the tax provision a company makes based on accounting income. It is a source of cash. It allows the company to delay paying part of its taxes until a later year.

Differences between tax and accounting procedures occur in many areas. These differences may be permanent or they may be "timing" differences. Permanent differences are ones that will never reverse and do not result in deferred taxes. For example, Canadian dividend income received by a company is considered income for accounting purposes. However, under the Income Tax Act these same dividends are generally not taxable. So there will be no tax expense reported on the financial statements, or on the company's tax form, since the dividends are permanently "tax-free." There are other examples of permanent differences, such as interest and penalties on taxes, which are not deductible for tax purposes but are considered expenses for accounting purposes.

Deferred taxes usually result from timing differences. The most common timing differences arise from the differences between book or financial depreciation of fixed assets, as already discussed, and capital cost allowances set in the income tax regulations. Capital

cost allowance is the income tax equivalent of depreciation, and allows for larger deductions during the early years of an asset's life. Tax provisions in the company's financial statements are calculated on book or financial statement income, whereas income tax payable in the year is calculated on income for tax purposes after deducting capital cost allowances. Financial depreciation is not deductible for income tax purposes. Capital cost allowances are deducted in its place. When financial tax provisions exceed taxes currently payable, the difference is a deferred tax credit (liability) on the company's balance sheet. The reverse is a deferred tax debit (asset) on the balance sheet.

Many other permanent and timing differences exist, including those related to inventory valuation, revenue recognition, leases, capital gains, allowable expenses, loss carryovers, warranties and business combinations. In each case, deferred income taxes on the balance sheet reflect the cumulative amount of these differences over the company's life. The current year's amount appears in the earnings statement, and shows the deferred taxes for that period, usually a year.

3. Minority Interest in Subsidiary Companies (item 19)

This item appears in some balance sheets that are consolidated. (*Consolidated* means that the parent company's figures are combined with those of its subsidiaries into a single joint statement.) Even if the parent company owns less than 100% of a subsidiary's stock, all of the assets and liabilities are combined in the consolidated financial statement. To compensate, the part not owned is shown in the consolidated balance sheet as minority interest. Minority interest, from the viewpoint of the consolidated statement, is considered to be the interest outsiders have in the subsidiary company. So it's seen as a quasi-liability which must be deducted in arriving at the consolidated shareholders' equity of the parent company.

4. Other Liabilities

Some companies use a section of the balance sheet between liabilities and shareholders' equity to set up provisions for estimated expected losses (e.g. from a lawsuit in progress against the company at balance sheet date, or as a result of investments in politically unstable countries). If this contingency is based solely on conservative thinking and refers to remote possibility rather than a specific loss in prospect, the amount is more properly included as a note to the financial statements.

5. Deferred Income

Deferred income results when a company gets paid for goods or services which it has not yet provided. Since the company has an obligation to deliver the goods or services in future, the unearned portion of the income represents a liability to the company, so it's shown as such. Deferred income is the opposite of a deferred charge, which appears on the asset side of the balance sheet.

A prepaid subscription to a magazine, covering future issues still unpublished when the payment was made, is deferred income, for example. These payments are deferred income to the magazine publisher. The amount would be shown as current or long-term, depending on the circumstances.

6. Long-Term (or "Funded") Debt (item 20)

This group of items finances the fixed assets on the other side of the balance sheet. Distinct from current debts which have to be paid within a year, the long-term debt of a company is usually due in monthly or annual instalments over several years, or in a lump sum in a future year. Any portion of long-term debt that is due in the next year is shown as a current item. The most common of these debts are mortgages, bonds and debentures though promissory notes and similar debt instrument types are common. Often, fixed assets have been pledged as security for these borrowings.

It's customary to describe these debt items on the balance sheet, or in a note attached to it, in enough detail to explain what kind of security is on the loan, the interest rate, when the debt becomes repayable and what sinking fund provision, if any, is made to pay it back. The sinking fund is the amount set aside each year for the debt's repayment. The money is usually given to a trustee who may either call in some of the debt securities for repayment, buy them on the open market for cancellation, or invest the funds in government securities to repay the debt at maturity.

Understanding Shareholders' Equity (items 21 to 25)

Items in this section represent the amount that shareholders have at risk in the business. The money that is paid in by the shareholders is designated as capital and the profits that have been earned over a period of years and not paid out as dividends make up the retained earnings. Another item called contributed surplus sometimes appears in this section. It, too, belongs to the shareholders, but originates from sources other than earnings. So the shareholders' equity section has the following items:

1. Share Capital (items 21 & 22)

This is the amount of money the company got for its shares when they were issued. So share capital shown on the balance sheet is not related in any way to the current market price of the outstanding shares. Share capital would not change from year to year unless the company issued new shares or bought back outstanding ones. Any excess received (when the shares were issued) over par or stated value is shown in contributed surplus.

2. Contributed Surplus (item 23)

Contributed surplus comes from sources other than earnings. An example is when a company sells its stock for more than its par value or, in the case of no par value shares, its stated value. So if a company's stock has a par value of $100 per share and is sold for $125 per share, the $100 is applied against the capital stock account, while the $25 difference goes into the contributed surplus account.

3. Retained Earnings (or Deficit) (item 24)

Retained Earnings is the portion of annual earnings retained by the company after payment of all expenses and the distribution of dividends. The earnings retained each year are reinvested in the business. The reinvestment of accumulated earnings may be held in cash or reinvested in other assets like inventories or property.

Retained earnings also serve as a cushion to absorb losses incurred in bad years. If a company has a loss in any year, the loss is deducted from the retained earnings. Each shareholder's ownership interest in the company would therefore be reduced. There would be less retained earnings from which dividend distributions can be made. If more losses than earnings accumulate, the resulting fig-ure is called a deficit.

4. Foreign Currency Translation Adjustments (item 25)

This item may appear in consolidated financial statements for companies with subsidiaries in foreign countries. These subsidiaries' assets are valued in the foreign country's currency where the company operates. If, due to a significant change in the exchange rate, the foreign assets are worth more (or less) at the time the consolidated balance sheet is prepared, this difference is included as an adjustment to shareholders' equity.

Example: Suppose a Canadian company owns a subsidiary in the United States, and the US dollar had risen dramatically since the subsidiary was purchased. The American company would be more valuable to the Canadian parent after the rise in the US dollar. The Canadian parent would show this increase as an addition to foreign currency translation adjustments under shareholders' equity.

THE EARNINGS STATEMENT

This statement – sometimes called the income statement or profit and loss statement or statement of revenue and expense – shows how much revenue a company got during the year selling its products or services, and its expenses for wages, materials, operating costs, taxes and other expense items. The difference between the two is the company's profit or loss for the year. The amount left over, after payment of income taxes, is net earnings, out of which dividends may be paid to the shareholders.

So the earnings statement reveals this about a company:

• Where the income comes from and how it is spent

• The adequacy of earnings both to assure the successful operation of the company and to provide income for the holders of its securities.

It should be stressed that, in analyzing a company's financial condition, its earning power is key. It's earnings power - how much and now consistently it can earn - that gives financial strength to a company and to its securities.Earnings power is shown by the earnings statement.

Structure of the Earnings Statement

Earnings statements all provide the same kind of financial information. But their make-up varies widely, not only among companies in different industries, but also among companies in the same industry. A condensed statement with only three, four or five items is inadequate. A more revealing statement may have 20 or 30 items. Most statements have 10 to 20 items. No matter how many items there are, they can be easily grouped in one of these four broad sections:

1. The operating section

2. The non-operating section

3. The creditors' section (relates to interest on items in creditors' section of the balance sheet)

4. The owners' section (relates to shareholders' equity in the balance sheet)

(The section headings would not normally appear as such in the earnings statement, but are included in the sample statement as a learning aid.)

Sections 1 and 2 show origin of income, sections 3 and 4 show its distribution.

A company generally has two main income sources. First, income from operations, i.e. the income from selling its main products or services. For example, if the company is a public utility, it derives its main income from the sale of gas or electricity. Such income is termed operating income – the income from its main operations.

The second income source isn't directly related to a company's normal operating activities. This income includes dividends and interest from investments, rents, royalties from processes or patents it owns, and sometimes profit from selling capital assets. Since income from these sources is not directly related to a company's main operations, it's called non-operating income.

If operating and non-operating income are combined in one figure in the earnings statement, it's impossible to uncover the company's real earning power. For example, a company might in one year realize a substantial profit from selling securities or some other asset. A profit of this kind is not likely to be repeated the next year. Yet if it were combined with operating income it would be impossible to see what the company's true earning power is, based on its main operations. Good accounting practice requires that operating income and non-operating income be shown separately in the earnings statement, especially if non-operating income is substantial.

The Operating Section

The operating section of the earnings statement may be readily divided into three parts:

- The operating income received by source
- The expense incurred to obtain that income
- The balance or net amount of that income (operating profit or loss)

The terminology used in describing income in the operating section is not always the same. Railroads and public utilities generally use the term operating revenue. In the case of an industrial concern, the comparable term is sales.

Net Sales (item 28)

The earnings statement of a commercial, mercantile or industrial company should start with the amount of net sales.

Net sales consists of gross sales less:

- Excise tax – applies to the oil, beverage and tobacco industries
- Returns and allowances – adjustments made because customers were sent unsatisfactory goods and returns of reusable containers
- Discounts – rebates on the sale price to customers for prompt payment

Net sales is a key figure in the earnings statement. It's the figure needed to calculate various ratios useful in determining the basic soundness of a company's financial position. For example, it must be known in order to calculate net and gross profit margins and average collection period. These ratios are used by credit managers, bankers and security analysts to investigate a company's financial affairs.

Cost of Goods Sold (item 29)

From the net sales figure, various operating expenses are deducted. These expenses arise in producing the income received from the sale of the company's products or services. The first such deduction, for a manufacturing or merchandising concern, is termed cost of goods sold. This item includes labor, raw materials, fuel and power, supplies and services, and other kinds of expenses which go directly into the manufacturing cost, or, for a merchandising concern, the cost of goods purchased for resale.

Gross Operating Profit (item 30)

Deducting the cost of goods sold figure from the amount of net sales produces another significant figure called gross operating profit. This figure is significant because it measures the margin of profit or spread between the cost of goods produced for sale and the net sales. When the percentage of gross operating profit to net sales is calculated and compared with those of other companies engaged in the same line of business, it provides an indication of whether the company's merchandising operations are more or less successful in producing profits than its competitors. Between different companies in the same business, differences in the margin of gross operating profit generally reflect differences in managerial ability, although they also can be caused by the inclusion of some expense items in the cost of goods sold of one company, and not in another.

Operating Expenses (items 31 to 33)

After gross operating profit has been determined, a number of other operating expense items are then deducted. The first is selling, general and administrative expenses. This item includes such expenses as office expenses, the cost of maintaining a sales organization and accounting staff, advertising expenses, and similar types of costs necessary to operate a business. Sometimes this item is combined with the cost of sales item and only one figure is shown to cover all these direct operating expenses. This practice is becoming less common as reporting standards improve.

The next item deducted is depreciation. Physical assets like automobiles, machinery, furniture, equipment and buildings depreciate with time and use. This is a cost of doing business and is deducted from operations. As assets are recorded on the basis of original cost, depreciation is simply the allocation of cost over the estimated useful life of the asset.

Adequate depreciation is of great importance to investors. That's why the Canadian Institute of Chartered Accountants (CICA) rules say it must be disclosed. The depreciation charge is a cost of goods sold if the related assets are used in the manufacturing process. If so, a note would be added to the statement indicating that treatment.

It is highly significant to the investor if the annual provision for depreciation is insufficient. In this event, the earnings of the company would be overstated and securities holders might find that the company was living off its capital or, in other words, not reinvesting sufficiently in plant and equipment to maintain operations. That's why the annual allowance and method of calculating depreciation should be carefully assessed. Even if accounting depreciation is adequate, however, the company may still be living off its capital.

Various other items properly regarded as operating expenses are also deducted in the operating section. These include contributions to employees' pension fund. Director's fees, remuneration of officers and legal fees may also be charged as separate expense items.

Net Operating Profit (or Loss) (item 34)

After deducting the total of all these operating expenses from the net sales figure, you reach the company's net operating profit for the period under review.

The Non-Operating Section

The earnings statement's non-operating section reveals the income received from various sources not directly related to the company's main operations. These include interest and dividends on securities held, rents from no-longer-required properties, royalties on patents, finance charges earned, etc.

With the exception of rental or financial income, there are few expenses tied to non-operating income. Such income is often included in sales and, therefore, distorts the sales figure for comparative purposes. So non-operating income must be excluded from sales before calculating ratios for comparison with other companies in the same industry.

A company may have a gain or loss in a year that's not expected to occur frequently, is not typical of normal business activity, and does not depend primarily on decisions by management or owners. A company may receive a "windfall-type" capital gain through an expropriation, or a loss resulting from a flood, earthquake or revolution, etc. This special gain or loss is usually stated as an extraordinary item on the earnings statement, after all other items of revenue and expense have been accounted for. (Another category – unusual items – results from events typical in the company's normal business activity even though caused by unusual circumstances, e.g. unusual bad debt or inventory losses.)

If extraordinary items were included in the company's income, it would distort results for the year. So companies report earnings both before and after extraordinary items. To make year-to-year comparisons meaningful, any calculations of a company's net earnings for a year should always be made before extraordinary items.

How a company distributes its income is shown in the earnings statement's final sections. Debtholders get interest payments on their securities or loans to the company, the government gets its share as tax, and shareholders rank next for dividends on their shares.

The Creditors' Section (items 37 and 38)

Income distributions to creditors are usually made as fixed interest charges to banks and other debtholders who have loaned money to the company. These interest charges are paid from income before taxes and are fixed in the sense that the amount of interest which has to be paid on borrowed money is definite. If the company has $1,000,000 worth of bonds outstanding in the hands of investors and these bonds bear 9% interest per annum, there's exactly $90,000 interest to be paid each year.

Interest charges are also fixed in the sense that they must be paid. Non-payment would result in default and give creditors the right to place the company in receivership. In the event of bankruptcy, the assets may be offered for sale and the proceeds used to pay off claims of the creditors. So to avoid receivership, these fixed charges must be paid before any of the income may be distributed to the shareholders. (Bank interest and debt interest, even taxes, may also be considered operating expenses since they're necessary costs of doing business.)

Subtracting fixed charges from total net income results in a figure which brings us to the statement's owners' section.

The Owners' Section

Taxes and Minority Interest (items 40 and 41)

The company's shareholders are its owners and are entitled to their net earnings share. Net earnings are total net income less creditors' charges and income taxes. Most companies show two types of income taxes: current and deferred. In consolidated statements for companies with minority interests, the minority interest portion of the subsidiary's earnings are deducted, since this doesn't belong to the parent company's shareholders.

Equity Income (item 42)

While minority interest results from the consolidation method of accounting, which is usually used when the parent owns more than 50% of the subsidiary's voting shares and consolidates both results into one financial statement, equity income is derived from the equity accounting method, and usually arises when 20% to 50% of the voting shares are owned. A third method, called the cost method, is mainly used when the ownership holding is under 20%.

Equity income arises when a parent company claims its share of a subsidiary's earnings. Let's assume Trans-Canada Retail Stores Ltd. owns 25% of Alberta Retail Stores Ltd., and that Alberta Retail Stores earned $20,000 (after tax) in a particular fiscal year. Trans-Canada Retail Stores, in its earnings statement, claims $5,000 (25%) of this as Equity Income. This item might also be called equity earnings, earnings from subsidiaries, or something similar.

Certain earnings calculations must be adjusted for equity income because, while the parent company claims this income, it does not actually receive it in cash. Equity income is a non-cash source of funds, just as depreciation, depletion, and amortization are non-cash uses of funds. Parent company earnings must be reduced by the equity income amount when calculating ratios where you need the company's cash earnings. You will note the inclusion of equity income in the ratios in the next section of this book.

If a subsidiary has a loss, the parent will claim its share of the loss on its earnings statement. This entry, called Equity Loss or something similar, reduces earnings on the parent's earnings statement. But, as with equity income, an equity loss is also a non-cash item. The equity loss would therefore have to be added back to the parent company's earnings when calculating ratios where a true picture of the company's cash earnings is needed

A related item – dividends from a subsidiary – is worth noting. Under the equity accounting method, dividends received by a

parent from its subsidiary aren't recorded in the parent's income statement. Instead, they're recorded in the statement of changes in financial position, perhaps as dividends from non-consolidated subsidiaries. Here, cash is actually received by the parent but is not included in the parent company's earnings as they appear on the earnings statement. Therefore, earnings calculations that are adjusted for equity income are sometimes also increased by the amount of dividends received from the subsidiary. Not all subsidiaries pay dividends, however. Equity income may appear on an income statement without a corresponding dividend entry on the statement of changes. Subsidiaries that do pay dividends don't always pay a significant amount per share. For these reasons, dividends appearing on the statement of changes aren't included in the ratios in the next section.

To sum up, the parent company records equity income which it did not actually receive in cash, and receives, in cash, dividends which it does not record as income. So cash earnings calculations should subtract equity income, and sometimes include any dividends received from the subsidiary.

The earnings statement finishes with net earnings (or deficit), the amount of profit from the year's operations that may be available for distribution to shareholders.

At this point net earnings are transferred to the retained earnings statement.

THE RETAINED EARNINGS STATEMENT

The profit or loss in a company's most recent year is determined in the earnings statement and then transferred to the *retained earnings statement*. Retained earnings are profits earned over the years that have not been paid to shareholders as dividends. These retained profits accrue to the shareholders, but the directors have decided to reinvest them in the business.

The retained earnings statement shows profits kept in the business year after year. Profit for the current year is added to, or the loss is subtracted from, the retained earnings balance from the prior year. Dividends paid during the year are subtracted in this statement.

This statement, then, shows earnings and dividends. But it's also used to record adjustments to past years' earnings. From time to time, amounts may be taken from retained earnings as a reserve against possible events such as a decline in the value of raw materials inventory bought when commodity prices were high. Whenever the term reserve is used on a federally-incorporated company's balance sheet, it describes an appropriation from retained earnings.

Using the term reserve doesn't mean a cash fund has been set aside. It just means that part of the retained earnings is unavailable to shareholders. Setting up a fund to meet some future contingency would need separate action by the board of directors. Establishing a reserve has limited usefulness, except to tell investors that the company has possible contingencies.

A new final retained earnings figure is calculated and carried to the balance sheet's shareholders' equity section. So the retained earnings statement is a link between the earnings statement and the balance sheet.

STATEMENT OF CHANGES IN FINANCIAL POSITION

While the balance sheet shows a company's financial position at a specific date, and the earnings statement summarizes the company's operating activities for the year, neither shows how the company's financial position changed from one period to the next. The statement of changes in financial position – also called the cash flow statement – fills this gap between the balance sheet and the income statement by providing information about how the company generated and spent its cash during the year.

The statement of changes in financial position helps users of financial statements to evaluate a company's liquidity and solvency, and in assessing it's ability to generate cash internally, to repay debts, to reinvest, and to pay dividends to shareholders. By reviewing cash flow statements over a number of years, you may see trends that might otherwise go unnoticed.

In the statement of changes in financial position, "cash" normally includes cash held in bank accounts, net of short term borrowings, and temporary investments. In some cases, other elements of working capital might be included when they are equivalent to cash. It is the changes in cash, and the reasons for them, that this financial statement shows.

A statement of changes in financial position shows the company's cash flows for the period under the following three headings:

Operating Activities is the company's net earnings adjusted for items such as depreciation, amortization and equity income, which do not involve an outlay or receipt of cash. Further adjustments are made for revenues and expenses which have not yet been realized as cash, such as accounts receivable and accounts payable.

Financing Activities include proceeds from issuing shares, funds received under long-term debt issues, long-term debt repayments and changes in term bank loans.

Investing Activities are cash outlays to acquire fixed assets, cash receipts on selling assets or investments, and income from investments when received as cash, etc.

OTHER INFORMATION IN THE ANNUAL REPORT

Notes to Financial Statements

There's plenty of detailed information shareholders need to know. But if it was all shown directly in the financial statements, they'd become too cluttered. So this information is usually shown in a series of notes. It's essential for an investor to read these notes and understand them. They offer important details about the company's financial condition. Items that are often included in a company's notes include accounting policies, description of fixed assets, share capital and long-term debt, commitments and contingencies.

Financial statements should also disclose information that shows significant segments of the company's operations first by industry and second by geographical area. The information for each segment should include revenue and profit and loss data, as well as capital expenditures and depreciation charges for the year, and identifiable assets at year end. An example is shown in Table 2.

The Auditor's Report

Canadian corporate law requires that every limited company appoint an auditor to represent shareholders and report

Table 2

PQR Corporation Limited – Segmented Results
thousands of dollars

| | Retailing | | Manufacturing | | Consolidated PQR Results | |
	Year 2	Year 1	Year 2	Year 1	Year 2	Year 1
Sales	$418,859	$395,515	$81,198	$67,921	$500,057	$463,436
Operating earnings	$ 25,557	$ 23,917	$ 5,124	$ 6,108	$ 30,025	$ 30,025
Interest (net)	–	–	–	–	$ 3,418	$ 8,708
Corporate charges	–	–	–	–	$ 3,821	$ 2,480
Earnings before income tax	–	–	–	–	$ 23,442	$ 18,837
Assets at year end	$121,090	$115,341	$43,271	$33,801	$164,361	$149,142
Capital expenditures and assets under capital leases for the period	$ 12,421	$ 8,149	$ 1,885	$ 1,184	$ 14,306	$ 9,333
Depreciation and amoritization	$ 8,714	$ 8,285	$ 1,318	$ 921	$ 10,032	$ 9,206

to them annually on the company's financial statements, and to express a written opinion on the statements' fairness and consistency. The auditor is appointed at the company's annual meeting by a shareholders' resolution and may be dismissed by them. A member of the Institute of Chartered Accountants in the province in which he or she carries on business may act as auditor. In some provinces, in addition to CAs, CGAs (Certified General Accountants) and CMAs (Certified Management Accountants) may also act as company auditors. In the United States, the CPA (Certified Public Accountant) fills the auditor's role.

Understanding Financial Statements

In Canada, the auditor's report has two paragraphs. The first describes the scope of the examination and will usually indicate that the examination was made in accordance with generally accepted auditing standards, and included those tests and procedures that the auditor considered necessary in the circumstances.

The second paragraph gives the auditor's opinion on the statements – indicating that the financial statements present fairly the financial position of the company, the results of the operations, and the changes in financial position for the period – in accordance with generally accepted accounting principles applied on a basis consistent with that of the preceding year.

Generally accepted accounting principles (GAAP) refer to the principles and practices to be used for recording and reporting business transactions issued by the Canadian Institute of Chartered Accountants. Where the CICA has not made it known what the accounting treatment for a particular matter should be, practice that's been generally accepted by the accounting profession and is in current use is considered appropriate. If there's any inconsistency in applying generally accepted accounting principles in a company's financial statements, reference is made to it in the auditor's report and to a note describing it in more detail.

The auditor may find that generally accepted accounting principles have not been used, or may be unable to form an opinion on one or more of the financial statements submitted to the shareholders. In that case, the auditor would state that he or she was unable to give any opinion whatsoever, or else include in the report his or her qualifications regarding the dubious items. A qualified report should be regarded as a signal that the financial statements may not present fairly the company's financial position or results of its operations. In some provinces, qualified reports are not allowed. Caution should be exercised by shareholders and investors in appraising the company's financial status.

Part 2

THE USE OF RATIOS

Now that you've learned what the financial statements reveal about a company's financial condition, the next step is to put that knowledge to work. We do that by testing the investment merits of the company's bonds and stocks.

The tool most commonly used to analyze financial statements is called a ratio. It is a relationship between two numbers, in which a number is usually related to 1, e.g. 2.2 to 1 or 2.2:1.

There are four types of ratios commonly used to analyze a company's financial statements:

Liquidity Ratios are used to judge the company's ability to meet its short-term commitments. An example is the working capital ratio, which shows the relationship between current assets and current liabilities.

Debt Ratios show how well the company can deal with its debt obligations. For example, the debt/equity ratio shows the relationship between the company's borrowing and the capital invested in it by shareholders.

Profitability Ratios illustrate how well management has made use of the company's resources. The net return on invested capital, for example, links the company's income with the invested capital responsible for producing it.

Value Ratios show the investor the worth of the company's shares or the return on owning them. An example is the price-earnings ratio which links a common share's market price to earnings per common share, allowing investors to compare a company's shares to others in the same industry.

Ratios are helpful but must be used with caution. One ratio alone does not tell much. Ratios are not proof but clues to help make a judgement. An unsatisfactory ratio might suggest an unfavorable condition. Or the conclusion that a company is financially strong may be confirmed by compiling a series of ratios.

Keep in mind that the significance of a ratio may vary between different types of companies. In analyzing an industrial company, for example, particular emphasis is laid upon the working capital ratio. In an electric utility company, however, it is not so important because there are no inventories of electric power since production is simultaneous with use. The power company's current assets are, therefore, low compared to a manufacturing company.

THE STUDY OF TRENDS

Ratios calculated from a company's financial statements for only one year have limited value. They become meaningful when compared with other ratios either internally, that is, with a series of similar ratios of the same company over a period, or externally, that is, with comparable ratios on similar companies or with industry averages.

Internal Trend Lines

A trend is shown by selecting a base date or period, treating the figure or ratio for that period as 100, and then dividing it successively into the comparable ratios for subsequent periods. The example on the following page shows this simple calculation for a typical pulp and paper company.

In the above example, 1991 is taken as the base year and the earnings per share for that year, $1.18, is treated as equivalent to 100. The trend ratios for later years are easily calculated by dividing $1.18 into earnings per share for each year and adjusting to 100.

A similar trend line over the same period for Pulp and Paper Company B is also shown on the following page.

Pulp and Paper Company A - Earnings per Share

Year	1991	1992	1993	1994	1995	1996	1997	1998	1999	2000
EPS	$1.18	$1.32	$1.73	$1.76	$1.99	$1.95	$2.04	$1.74	$1.86	$2.04
	$1.18	$1.32	$1.73	$1.76	$1.99	$1.95	$2.04	$1.74	$1.86	$2.04
	$1.18	$1.18	$1.18	$1.18	$1.18	$1.18	$1.18	$1.18	$1.18	$1.18
Trend	100	112	147	149	169	165	173	147	158	173

Pulp and Paper Company B - Earnings per Share

Year	1991	1992	1993	1994	1995	1996	1997	1998	1999	2000
EPS	$0.71	$0.80	$0.90	$0.94	$1.02	$0.96	$0.92	$0.72	$0.60	$0.64
	$0.71	$0.80	$0.90	$0.94	$1.02	$0.96	$0.92	$0.72	$0.60	$0.64
	$0.71	$0.71	$0.71	$0.71	$0.71	$0.71	$0.71	$0.71	$0.71	$0.71
Trend	100	113	127	132	144	135	130	101	85	90

The trend line for each company shown above reflects the characteristic earnings fluctuations typical for pulp and paper companies. Adding new pulp or newsprint machines often causes temporary overcapacity and reduces earnings until demand catches up with supply. The trend line for Company B suggests some overcapacity in recent years as earnings show a decline.

Advantages of Trend Ratios

The trend-ratio method is useful because changes in items are clearly brought out. It is also much simpler arithmetically and lends itself to clearer interpretation than the alternative two-step method of calculating percentage changes from year to year.

Disadvantages

A trend line will be misleading if the base period is not truly representative. It is also impossible to apply the method if the base period figure is negative, i.e. if a loss was sustained in the base year.

External Comparisons

Ratios are useful for comparing financial results where the companies are in the same or similar industries (e.g. a distiller with a brewer). The difference brought out by the trend lines is revealing not only in putting each company's earnings per share in historical perspective, but also in showing how each has fared in relation to the other.

In external comparisons, not only should the companies be similar in operation, but the basis used to calculate each ratio compared should be the same. It is misleading, for example, to compare inventory turnover ratios (discussed later) of two companies where one calculation uses "cost of goods sold" and the other "net sales." This comparison would be inaccurate since the calculation basis is different.

Industry ratios are also useful as a standard against which individual companies' performance may be conveniently measured. Industry ratios are available from Dun & Bradstreet, the Canadian Manufacturers' Association and some chartered banks. A good example for industry comparison is net earnings to shareholders' equity. By comparing this figure for a particular company with the appropriate industry average, stockholders and management can check their company's performance against the industry as a whole.

Over the years, analysts accumulate knowledge of industries and companies from interviews with industry and corporate managements, and by studying corporate annual reports and other statistics.

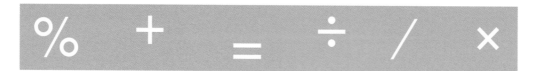

They draw on industry ratios, analyze each ratio's components and apply arithmetical rule-of-thumb tests. This helps them get expertise to draw on in interpreting ratios and trends through their close familiarity with industries and companies. You may be able to accumulate such knowledge with continued industry study over time. You can, in any event, interpret the ratios that follow and apply them in assessing securities' merits.

To make it easier to follow and understand how ratios are calculated, items used in the following examples are numbered to correspond to the relative items in Trans-Canada Retail Stores Ltd.'s sample financial statements.

The following is a list of ratios by type:

Ratios to Analyze Liquidity

- Working Capital Ratio (or Current Ratio)
- Quick Ratio (The Acid Test)

Ratios to Analyze Debt

- Asset Coverage
- Percentage of Total Capital Ratios
- Debt/Equity Ratio
- Cash Flow/Debt
- Interest Coverage
- Preferred Dividend Coverage

Ratios to Analyze Profitability

- Gross Profit Margin
- Operating Profit Margin

- Net Profit Margin
- Pre-Tax Return on Invested Capital
- Net Return on Invested Capital
- Net Return on Equity
- Inventory Turnover

Ratios to Analyze Value

- Percentage of Available Earnings Paid Out as Preferred and Common Dividends
- Percentage of Available Earnings Paid Out as Common Dividends
- Earnings per Common Share
- Dividend Yield
- Price-Earnings Ratio
- Equity per Preferred Share
- Equity per Common Share

ANALYZING LIQUIDITY

L iquidity ratios help the investor evaluate a company's ability to turn assets into cash to meet its short-term obligations. For a company to remain solvent, it must be able to meet its current liabilities. So it must have an adequate amount of working capital.

Working Capital Ratio or Current Ratio

By subtracting total current liabilities from total current assets, we obtain the company's working capital, also referred to as net current assets. The working capital for Trans-Canada Retail would be calculated as follows:

Current Assets (item 6)	$12,238,000
Less: Current Liabilities (item 17)	$ 4,410,000
Equals: Working Capital	$ 7,828,000

This relationship is often expressed in terms of a ratio. In this example, the working capital ratio would be expressed as follows:

Working Capital Ratio

$$\frac{\text{Current assets}}{\text{Current liabilities}} \quad \text{or} \quad \frac{\text{Item 6}}{\text{Item 17}} = \frac{\$12,238,000}{\$ 4,410,000} = 2.78{:}1$$

We saw earlier that current assets are cash and other company possessions that can be readily turned into cash (and normally would be) within one year. Current liabilities are the opposite. They are liabilities of the company due and payable within one year. In our example, the company has $2.78 of cash and equivalents to pay every $1 of current liabilities.

Is this good or bad or so-so? It depends on many factors such as type of business, composition of current assets, inventory turnover rate and credit terms. A current ratio of 2:1 is good, but not exceptional, because it means there is $2 cash and equivalents to pay each $1 of debt. However, if Company A had 50% cash in its current assets and Company B had 90% inventories, and each had a current ratio of 2:1, Company A would be better than B because it would be more liquid and could pay its current debts more easily and quickly. Also, if a cur-rent ratio of 2:1 is good, is 20:1 ten times as good? No. If a company's current ratio exceeds 5:1 and consistently maintains such a high level, the company may have too much cash accumulated which could indicate sales problems (too much inventory) or financial mismanagement.

Importance of Working Capital

A company's ability to meet its obligations, expand its sales, and take advantage of financial opportunities as they arise is, to an important degree, determined by its working capital position. Insufficient working capital and inability to liquidate current assets readily are common reasons why businesses fail.

Different businesses have different working capital requirements. In some businesses (e.g. distilleries), several years may pass before raw materials are processed and sold as finished products. So these businesses need significant working capital available to finance operations until cash comes from selling finished products. In others (e.g. meat packers), the manufacturing process is much shorter and cash from sales is received more quickly and is more readily available for paying current debts. These businesses can safely operate with less working capital.

Rather than relying on rules of thumb, well-managed companies prepare a cash forecast. This enables the company to predict its cash needs in advance and to plan a way to meet these needs in an orderly fashion.

Quick Ratio (The Acid Test)

The second of the two common corporate liquidity ratios, the quick ratio, is a more stringent test than the current ratio. In this calculation, inventories, which are generally not a very liquid asset, are subtracted from current assets. The quick ratio shows how well current liabilities are covered by cash and by items with a ready cash value.

Current assets include inventories which, at times, may be difficult to convert into cash readily or, due to changing market conditions, may be carried on the balance sheet at what may turn out to be inflated values. There is, however, a more conservative way to test a company's ability to meet its current obligations: the quick ratio.

Quick Ratio

Formula $\dfrac{\text{Current assets - inventories}}{\text{Current liabilities}}$

Example $\dfrac{\text{Item 6 - Item 4}}{\text{Item 17}}$ or $\dfrac{\$12,238,000 - \$9,035,000}{\$4,410,000} = \dfrac{\$3,203,000}{\$4,410,000} = 0.73{:}1$

Quick assets are current assets less inventories. In this example, the ratio is 0.73 to 1, which means there are 73 cents of current assets, not counting inventories, to meet each $1 of current liabilities.

There's no absolute standard for this ratio, but if it's 1 to 1 or better it suggests a good liquid position. However, companies with a quick ratio of less than 1 to 1 may be just as good if they have a high rate of inventory turnover. Why? Because inventory that's turned over quickly is the equivalent of cash. In our example, however, a quick ratio of 0.73:1 is probably satisfactory since our company is a retail store chain – an industry characterized by large inventories which have a high turnover rate.

ANALYZING DEBT

T he analysis of a company's debt lets investors judge how well the company can deal with its debt obligations. Excessive borrowing increases the company's costs as it must service the debt by paying interest on the outstanding bank loans, notes payable, bond and/or debenture issues.

If a company can't generate enough cash to pay the interest on its outstanding debt, then it could be forced into bankruptcy by its creditors. If the company must sell off its assets to meet these obligations, then investors who have purchased bonds, debentures, or stock in the company could lose some or all of their investment.

Asset Coverage

This ratio shows the net tangible assets of the company per $1,000 of total debt outstanding. It lets the debtholder measure protection provided by the company's tangible assets (i.e. all assets less intangibles such as goodwill and similar items) after all prior liabilities have been met.

Assets valued well in excess of a company's debt are normally needed to generate the earnings necessary to meet interest requirements and repay debt. At the same time, asset coverage shows the amount of assets (at book values) backing the debt securities. However, at best, asset values should be treated with extreme caution: The realizable value of assets in liquidation could be substantially less than their book values when the company is a going concern.

Again, asset values are usually calculated over a number of years to see the trend.

It's important for a debtholder to know the asset value behind each $1,000 of total debt outstanding. Normally, the debtholder

has a claim against all the company's assets after providing for liability items which rank ahead of his or her claim. To be conservative, deferred charges and intangible assets such as goodwill and patents are first deducted from the total asset figure. In our example, there's $5,424 in assets backing each $1,000 of total debt outstanding after providing for current liabilities other than bank advances, and the current portion of long-term debt, both being included in total debt outstanding. Trans-Canada Retail Stores Ltd. therefore meets the minimum rule of thumb standard for industrials by having at least $2,000 of assets behind each $1,000 of debt (see below).

In this and most other rules of thumb, the minimums are less for utilities than for industrials because utilities have a more stable source of income than most industrials. They are characterized by heavy investment in permanent property, which accounts for a large part of their total assets, and are subject to regulation which ensures the utility a fair return on its investment in its facilities. So, there's a greater degree of earnings' stability and continuity than for industrials.

Rules of Thumb for Net Tangible Assets behind Total Debt Outstanding

• *Utilities* – At least $1,500 of net tangible assets per $1,000 of total debt outstanding.

• *Industrials* – At least $2,000 of net tangible assets per $1,000 of total debt outstanding.

This calculation uses book values, and these usually have no relationship to current market values, especially for fixed assets. Also, the fixed assets, except for land, may have no value except to a continuing business, so it would be pointless to sell them to satisfy debtholders. Because of these limitations, some rating services consider this ratio only of academic interest. It's important to know, however, because in some provinces (e.g. Ontario) it's a legal requirement that this ratio be disclosed in prospectuses for most new debt issues.

Analyzing Financial Statements

Asset Coverage

Formula

$$\frac{\text{Total assets} - \text{deferred charges} - \text{intangible assets} - \text{current liabilities}}{\text{Total debt outstanding (i.e. short-term debt + long-term debt) } / \$1,000}$$

less short-term debt such as bank advances and the current portion of long-term debt

Note: The debtholder's claim on assets ranks prior to deferred income taxes and minority interest.

Example

$$\frac{\text{Item 11} - \text{Item 9} - \text{Item 10} - [\text{Item 17 less (Item 12} + \text{Item 16)}]}{(\text{Item 12} + \text{Item 16} + \text{Item 20}) / \$1,000}$$

$$\frac{\$19,761,000 - \$136,000 - \$150,000 - [\$4,410,000 \text{ less } (\$1,630,000 + \$120,000)]}{(\$1,630,000 + \$120,000 + \$1,350,000) / \$1,000}$$

or $\quad \dfrac{\$16,815,000}{3,100} = \$5,424$ per $1,000 total debt outstanding

Our sample company, Trans-Canada Retail Stores Ltd., has only one issue of long-term debt outstanding (item 20). So calculating net tangible assets (NTA) per $1,000 of total debt outstanding is, accordingly, fairly straightforward. If more than one issue were outstanding, the NTA coverage calculation would include that debt figure as well, but of course the senior issue would be better covered than a junior issue. The senior issue has higher priority in interest and liquidation proceeds.

Percentage of Total Capital Ratios

These ratios simply show what percentage of total invested capital each type of contributor provided, or is entitled to. (A percentage is equivalent to a ratio in which a number is related to 100. Thus, 46% is the same as the ratio 46:100 or 0.46:1.) The common shareholders

Percentage of Total Capital Ratios

Formula

Short-term debt	Item 12	$ 1,630,000
+Item 16	+Item 16	$ 120,000
+ Long-term debt	+Item 20	$ 1,350,000
+ Par value of preferred shares	+Item 21	$ 750,000
Common equity		
+ Stated value of common shares	+Item 22	$ 1,564,000
+ Contributed surplus	+Item 23	$ 150,000
+ Retained earnings	+Item 24	$ 10,835,000
+ Foreign exchange adjustment	+Item 25	$ 60,000
= Invested capital		$16,459,000

Percentage of capital structure attributable to debtholders (short and long-term):

Example

$$\frac{\text{Item 12 + Item 16 + Item 20}}{\text{Invested capital}} \times 100$$

or

$$\frac{\$1,630,000 + \$120,000 + \$1,350,000}{\$16,459,000} \times 100$$

$$\frac{\$3,100,000}{\$16,459,000} \times 100 = 18.83\% \text{ (Debtholders — short and long-term)}$$

Percentage of capital structure attributable to preferred shareholders:

$$\frac{\text{Item 21}}{16,459,000} \times 100$$

or

$$\frac{\$750,000}{\$16,459,000} \times 100 = 4.56\% \text{ (Preferred shareholders)}$$

Percentage of capital structure attributable to common shareholders:

$$\frac{\text{Item 22 + Item 23 + Item 24 + Item 25}}{16,459,000} \times 100$$

$$\frac{\$1,564,000 + \$150,000 + \$10,835,000 + \$60,000}{\$16,459,000} \times 100$$

$$\frac{\$12,609,000}{\$16,459,000} \times 100 = 76.61\% \text{ (Common shareholders)}$$

are usually entitled to more than they provided because retained earnings accumulate to their credit over the years. Long-term debtholders and preferred shareholders are either entitled to par value or par plus a small premium.

These balance sheet relationships help determine how sound a company's capitalization is. In our example, 18.83% of the capital structure is in short and long-term debt, 4.56% is in preferred stock, and the balance of 76.61% is in common equity. A high proportion of debt in the capitalization may mean that the company will have trouble meeting heavy interest and sinking fund charges when earnings are low. On the other hand, if a company can earn a higher return on its invested capital than its cost to borrow, it's good financial management to have a debt component in the capital structure. Use of debt can expand the size of the company with resulting benefits.

Unfortunately, there is no general rule to determine what is an acceptable capitalization. The relationship of debt to total capitalization varies widely for companies in different industries. It's normal for public utility, pipeline and real estate companies, for example, to have a fairly substantial proportion of their capital structure as debt. But if a company engaged in manufacturing products subject to wide fluctuation in demand showed a debt ratio as high as that for public utilities, the soundness of its capital structure would be questioned. Although what is acceptable capitalization is somewhat intuitive, the following rules of thumb provide a rough guide and are consistent with the more specific debt/equity requirements covered next.

Rules of Thumb for Capital Structure

• *Utilities* – Total debt outstanding shouldn't exceed 60% of total capital, taking the equity component at book value.

• *Industrials* – Total debt outstanding shouldn't exceed one-third of total capital, taking the equity component at book value.

Debt/Equity Ratio

This ratio pinpoints the relationship of debt to equity and can be a warning that a company's borrowing is excessive. The higher the debt/equity ratio, the higher the financial risk. Too large a debt burden reduces the margin of safety behind the debtholder's capital, increases the company's fixed charges, reduces earnings available for dividends and, in times of recession or high interest rates, could cause a financial crisis.

In the example below, the debt/equity ratio is 23.21% (0.23:1).

Rules of Thumb for Debt/Equity Ratio

• *Utilities* – Total debt outstanding should not be more than one and a half times the book value of shareholders' equity, that is, the numerator (or first number in the ratio) should not exceed 1.5 (150%).

• *Industrials* – Total debt outstanding should not be more than half the book value of shareholders' equity, that is, the numerator

---

Debt/Equity Ratio

Formula

$$\frac{\text{Total debt outstanding (i.e. short* and long-term)}}{\text{Book value of shareholders' equity}}$$

* In this example, bank advances and first mortgage bonds due within one year.

Example

$$\frac{\text{Item 12 + Item 16 + Item 20}}{\text{Item 21 + Item 22 + Item 23 + Item 24 + Item 25}}$$

$$\frac{\$1,630,000 + \$120,000 + \$1,350,000}{\$750,000 + \$1,564,000 + \$150,000 + \$10,835,000 + \$60,000}$$

$$= \frac{\$3,100,000}{\$13,359,000} \times 100 = 23.21\% \ (0.23{:}1)$$

(or first number in the ratio) should not exceed 0.5 (50%).

The preceding calculation shows the Trans-Canada Retail Stores Ltd.'s debt/equity ratio of 0.23:1 (23.21%) is acceptable since it does not exceed the 0.5:1 (50%) rule of thumb.

Cash Flow/Total Debt Outstanding

This is an important ratio because it gauges a company's ability to repay funds it borrowed. Since bank advances are short-term and require repayment (or rollover) normally within a year, and corporate debt issues commonly have sinking funds requiring annual cash outlays, a company's annual cash flow should be adequate to meet these commitments.

Before calculating this ratio, it is important to define cash flow and consider its significance.

Cash flow is a company's net earnings plus all deductions not requiring a cash outlay, such as depreciation and deferred income taxes, less all additions not received in cash, such as equity income.

Because of the huge size of non-cash deductions on earnings statements (items like operating charges which do not involve an actual cash outlay) cash flow often gives a broader earnings power picture than net earnings alone. So it's a better indicator for ability to pay dividends and finance expansion. It's particularly useful when comparing companies in the same industry in these areas. It can reveal the ability of a company showing little or no net earnings after depreciation and write-offs to meet its debts.

Companies often have to meet liabilities not shown as expense items on the earnings statement, e.g. sinking fund payments or outstanding commitments for capital assets. So cash flow, particularly when used in isolation as "cash flow per share," may be misleading.

Using cash flow properly requires that it be considered in relation

to a company's total financial requirements, as shown by its financial statements, including the statement of changes in financial position. The latter puts cash flow in perspective as a source of funds available to meet financial requirements.

A relatively high cash flow to debt ratio is considered positive and, conversely, a low ratio is negative. Analysts set minimum standards to judge debt repayment capacity which help give another perspective for evaluating debt.

Here are suggested standards to assess debt repayment capacity:

Rules of Thumb for Debt Repayment Capacity

• *Utilities* – Annual cash flow in each of the last five fiscal years should be at least 20% (0.20:1) of total debt outstanding in each respective year.

• *Industrials* – Annual cash flow in each of the last five fiscal years should be at least 30% (0.30:1) of total debt outstanding in each respective year.

Cash Flow/Total Debt Outstanding

Formula

$$\frac{\begin{array}{c}\text{Net earnings (before extraordinary items) − equity income} \\ \text{+ minority interest in earnings of subsidiary companies} \\ \text{+ deferred income taxes + depreciation + any other} \\ \text{deductions not paid out in cash, e.g. depletion, amortization etc.}\end{array}}{\text{Total debt outstanding (i.e. short and long-term)}} \times 100$$

Example

$$\frac{\text{Item 43 − Item 42 + Item 41 + Item 40 (deferred portion only) + Item 32}}{\text{Item 12 + Item 16 + Item 20}} \times 100$$

$$= \frac{\$1,086,000 - \$5,000 + \$12,000 + \$50,000 + \$556,000}{\$1,630,000 + \$120,000 + \$1,350,000} \times 100$$

$$= \frac{\$1,699,000}{\$3,100,000} \times 100 = 54.81\% \ (0.55:1)$$

The calculation shows that Trans-Canada Retail Stores Ltd.'s cash flow/debt ratio is 0.55:1, which is acceptable since it exceeds the 0.30:1 rule of thumb.

It's usual to calculate the cash flow to total debt outstanding ratio for each of the last five fiscal years. An improving trend is desirable. A declining trend usually indicates a weakening in financial strength unless individual ratios for each year are far in excess of minimum standards. For example, if the latest year's ratio was 0.61 (Year 5) and preceding years' ratios were 0.60 (Year 4), 0.63 (Year 3), 0.65 (Year 2) and 0.70 (Year 1), there would seem to be no cause for concern because each year's ratio is strong.

Interest Coverage

This ratio tests a company's ability to pay the interest charges on its debt, and indicates how many times these charges are covered based on earnings available to pay them. Interest coverage indicates a safety margin, since a company's inability to meet its interest charges could result in bankruptcy.

It's essential to take into account all interest charges, whether on bank loans, short-term debt, senior debt or junior debt. A default on any of them immediately impairs the issuer's ability to meet its obligations on the others, and can result in a default.

If new debt has been issued by the company during the year, interest on the new debt will be payable only for that period the debt has been outstanding. Conservative practice is to allow for a full year's interest on the new debt in the interest coverage calculation. However, this may be too conservative since the funds borrowed from the debt issue have been at work for the company only for the period as that interest has been payable. For this reason, it's acceptable to use the published interest charges figure, i.e. the actual amount incurred during the year.

Interest coverage is generally considered to be the most important measurable or quantitative test. An earnings level well above interest requirements is deemed necessary as protection for possible adverse conditions in future years. The greater the coverage, the greater the safety margin.

To assess coverage adequacy, it's common to set criteria – for example, that an industrial company's annual interest requirements in each of the last five years be covered at least three times by earnings available for interest payment in each year. At this level, its debt securities would be considered as acceptable investment quality.

A company may fail to meet the coverage standards, but never experience any problem paying all its debt obligations. However, the securities of such a company are considered a much higher risk because they lack an acceptable safety margin. So the interest coverage standards only help suggest whether a company will be able to meet its interest obligations.

Interest Coverage

Formula

$$\frac{\text{Net earnings (before extraordinary items)} - \text{equity income} + \text{minority interest in earnings of subsidiary companies} + \text{all income taxes} + \text{total interest charges}}{\text{Total interest charges}}$$

Example

$$\frac{\text{Item 43} - \text{Item 42} + \text{Item 41} + \text{Item 40} + \text{Item 37} + \text{Item 38}}{\text{Item 37} + \text{Item 38}}$$

$$\frac{\$1,086,000 - \$5,000 + \$12,000 + \$880,000 + \$120,700 + \$168,300}{\$120,700 + \$168,300}$$

$$\frac{\$2,262,000}{\$289,000} = 7.83 \text{ times}$$

Analyzing Financial Statements

The year-to-year trend in the interest coverage calculation is also important. Ideally, an improving trend is desirable, with a company not only meeting the coverage standards each year, but also increasing its coverage over the period. A stable trend which meets the minimum standards, but shows a little variation over the period, is also considered acceptable. But a deteriorating trend suggests further analysis is required to determine if the company's financial position has seriously weakened. Aberrations in the trend may occur, for example, resulting from a long strike. That may cause a big drop in earnings in a single year, but will not likely hurt the company's basic financial soundness seriously in later years.

Normally an assessment of bond quality allows for both good and bad times by providing the safety margin judged necessary for a company to weather difficult economic conditions and pay its debt. A company that is conservatively financed and in a strong financial position will likely encounter no problems.

However, a steep decline in earnings, particularly if prolonged or caused by a fundamental deterioration in the company's financial position, should prompt a revaluation of the debt issue's quality. A sudden reversal from a profit to a loss position also merits close scrutiny. Other factors such as a rapid build-up in short-term bank loans could also change the investment calibre of a company's debt securities. So continuous monitoring is necessary to ensure that current developments don't adversely affect the ability to meet debt obligations.

The calculation above shows that Trans-Canada Retail Stores Ltd.'s interest charges for the year were covered approximately 7.83 times by net income available to pay them. Stated another way, it had $7.83 of net income from which to pay every $1 of interest.

There are no set rules on what coverage is acceptable. It varies not only for companies in different industries, but also for companies in the same industry depending on their past earnings records and future prospects. The past record of a company's interest coverage is particularly important, because a company must meet its fixed charges both in good times and bad. Unless it's demonstrated its ability to do so it can't be said to meet the test.

The following rules of thumb, however, are generally regarded as acceptable standards:

Rules of Thumb for Interest Coverage

• *Utilities* – Total annual interest payments in each of the last five fiscal years should be covered at least two times by earnings available in each respective year.

• *Industrials* – Total annual interest payments in each of the last five fiscal years should be covered at least three times by earnings available in each respective year.

For utility companies, a high interest coverage ratio is not required. Such companies usually have a license to operate in specific areas with little or no competition, and rate boards establish rates which enable them to earn a fair return on their capital investment. By contrast, industrial companies' earnings are likely to be more volatile, so a higher coverage ratio is desirable to provide a bigger safety margin.

In addition to meeting the stated arithmetical minimums in each of the last five fiscal years, companies should show a steady or rising trend in their year-to-year earnings available for interest charges, and in their year-to-year interest coverage figures over the same period. A weakening or declining pattern is usually a danger signal.

Preferred Dividend Coverage

Similar to interest coverage, this ratio indicates the margin of safety behind preferred dividends. It's essentially an extension of the interest coverage calculation to include preferred dividends. It's sometimes called the prior charges method because the coverage calculation includes all prior fixed charges, i.e. bank and other debt interest, in addition to preferred dividends.

Since preferred issues are junior to debt issues, the rules of thumb that apply when a company has both preferred and debt outstanding should certainly be no less than those that apply when only debt is outstanding. In practice, the same rules of thumb are applied whether only debt is outstanding or both debt and preferreds are outstanding.

Preferred Dividend Coverage

Formula

$$\frac{\text{Net earnings (before extraordinary items)} - \text{equity income} + \text{minority interest in earnings of subsidiary companies} + \text{all income taxes} + \text{total interest charges}}{\text{Total interest charges} + \text{preferred dividend payments before tax}}$$

Example

$$\frac{\text{Item 43} - \text{Item 42} + \text{Item 41} + \text{Item 40} + \text{Item 37} + \text{Item 38}}{\text{Item 37} + \text{Item 38} + \text{Item 47 (before tax)}}$$

$$\frac{\$1{,}086{,}000 - \$5{,}000 + \$12{,}000 + \$880{,}000 + \$120{,}700 + \$168{,}300}{\$120{,}700 + \$168{,}300 + \dfrac{(\$37{,}500 \times 100)}{(100 - 44.60)}}$$

$$\frac{\$2{,}262{,}00}{\$289{,}000 + \$67{,}690} = \frac{\$2{,}262{,}000}{\$356{,}690} = 6.34 \text{ times}$$

Apparent Tax Rate

Since preferred dividends are paid after income tax, the coverage is calculated on a pre-tax basis by adjusting the preferred dividends for income tax. To make this adjustment, the preferred dividend figure is adjusted by the approximate percentage rate of income tax – known as the apparent tax rate – that a company paid for the year. Because of the differences in figures that companies report in their income tax returns and in their annual reports, the apparent tax rate is not usually the actual tax rate of the company, but merely an approximate rate for analytical purposes.

An example of the calculation of Trans-Canada Retail Stores' apparent tax rate follows:

$$\frac{\text{Current and deferred income taxes}}{\substack{\text{Net earnings before extraordinary items} \\ \text{– equity income + minority interest in} \\ \text{earnings of subsidiary companies} \\ \text{+ current and deferred income taxes}}} \times 100$$

$$\frac{\text{Item 40}}{\text{Item 43 – Item 42 + Item 41 – Item 40}} \times 100$$

or

$$\frac{\$880,000}{\$1,086,000 - \$5,000 + \$12,000 + \$880,000} \times 100$$

$$= \quad \frac{\$880,000}{\$1,973,000} \times 100 \quad = 44.60\%$$

So an after-tax dividend of \$55.40 would be equivalent to a before-tax dividend of \$100 (\$100 gross dividend – \$45.60 tax = \$55.40 after-tax dividend).

Thus:
$$\frac{\$55.40 \text{ after tax dividend}}{\$100 \text{ gross dividend}} = \frac{\$37,500 \text{ after-tax dividend}}{\$ X \text{ gross dividend}}$$

$$55.40 \, X = \$3,750.000$$

$$X = \frac{\$3,750,000}{55.40} = \$67,690 \text{ grossed-up (i.e. theoretical) dividend}$$

A simple formula for grossing-up preferred dividends:

$$\text{After-tax dividends} \quad \times \quad \frac{100}{100 - \text{Apparent tax rate}}$$

Rules of Thumb for Preferred Dividend Coverage

• *Utilities* – The combined debt and preferred charges in each of the last five fiscal years should be covered at least two times by earnings available in each respective year.

• *Industrials* – The combined debt and preferred charges in each of the last five fiscal years should be covered at least three times by earnings available in each respective year.

Trans-Canada Retail Stores Ltd.'s preferred coverage therefore is well above the minimum requirement (6.34 times versus three times).

As with interest coverage, the year-to-year trend, as well as the results in each of the last five fiscal years, should be examined to see if there's a weakening or improving pattern.

Our specimen company, Trans-Canada Retail Stores Ltd., has only one preferred share issue outstanding (Item 21). If more than one issue were outstanding, the calculation would be similar, but total preferred dividends would be used, even if the intention was to assess one particular issue.

In the case of companies having only preferred issues and no debt, the preferred coverage after tax (net earnings available for preferred dividends/annual preferred dividend requirements) should meet the same minimum requirements as companies with both preferred and debt.

ANALYZING PROFITABILITY

T he analysis of a company's earnings tells the investor how well management is using the company's resources.

Gross Profit Margin

This ratio, as well as the operating and net profit margin ratios, is useful both for internal trend lines and external comparisons, especially in industries such as food products and cosmetics where turnover is high and competition severe. The gross margin is an indication of management's efficiency in turning over the company's goods at a profit. It shows the company's rate of profit after allowing for the cost of goods sold. See calculation below.

Gross Profit Margin

Formula

$$\frac{\text{Net sales} - \text{cost of goods sold}}{\text{Net sales}} \times 100$$

Example

$$\frac{\text{Item 28} - \text{Item 29}}{\text{Item 28}} \times 100$$

or

$$\frac{\$43,800,000 - \$28,250,000}{\$43,800,000} \times 100$$

$$= \frac{\$15,550,000}{\$43,800,000} \times 100 = 35.50\%$$

Operating Profit Margin

In computing this ratio for companies subject to excise taxes, e.g. tobacco companies, it is important that the net sales figure used in the calculation is "net sales after excise taxes."

This ratio is a more stringent measure of the company's ability to manage its resources as it also takes into account the selling, general, and administrative expenses incurred in producing earnings. One advantage is that it allows profit margin comparison between companies which do not show "cost of goods sold" as a separate figure and for which, consequently, gross profit margin cannot be calculated.

Operating Profit Margin

Formula

$$\frac{\text{Net sales} - (\text{cost of goods sold} + \text{selling, administrative and general expenses})}{\text{Net sales}} \times 100$$

Example

$$\frac{\text{Item 28} - (\text{Item 29} + \text{Item 31})}{\text{Item 28}} \times 100$$

or

$$\frac{\$43,800,000 - (\$28,250,000 + \$12,752,000)}{\$43,800,000} \times 100$$

$$= \frac{\$43,800,000 - \$41,002,000}{\$43,800,000} \times 100$$

$$= \frac{\$2,798,000}{\$43,800,000} \times 100 = 6.39\%$$

Net Profit Margin

Net profit margin is an important indicator showing how efficiently the company is managed after taking into account both expenses and taxes. This ratio is the end result for the period. It effectively sums up in a single figure management's ability to run the business.

To be comparable from company to company and year to year, net profit must be shown before minority interest has been deducted and

equity income added, since not all companies have these items. The sales figure used in this calculation should be net of excise taxes.

Net Profit Margin

Formula

$$\frac{\text{Net earnings (before extraordinary items)} - \text{equity income} + \text{minority interest in earnings of subsidiary companies}}{\text{Net sales}} \times 100$$

Example

$$\frac{\text{Item 43} - \text{Item 42} + \text{Item 41}}{\text{Item 28}} \times 100$$

or

$$\frac{\$1,086,000 - \$5,000 + \$12,000}{\$43,800,000} \times 100$$

$$= \frac{\$1,093,000}{\$43,800,000} \times 100 = 2.50\%$$

Pre-Tax Return on Invested Capital

This ratio on the opposite page correlates income with the invested capital responsible for producing it, without reference to whether creditors or owners provided the capital. In other words, this ratio shows how well management has employed the assets at its disposal.

Net (or After-Tax) Return on Invested Capital

The differences between this ratio and the previous one are that income tax is not included in the numerator in this case, and total interest charges after tax, instead of total interest charges, are added to net earnings (before extraordinary items).

Analyzing Financial Statements

Pre-Tax Return on Invested Capital

Formula

$$\frac{\text{Net earnings (before extraordinary items)} + \text{income taxes} + \text{total interest charges}}{\text{Invested capital*}} \times 100$$

*The components of this item were discussed on page 50.

Example

$$\frac{\text{Item 43} + \text{Item 40} + \text{Item 37} + \text{Item 38}}{\text{Item 12} + \text{Item 16} + \text{Item 20} + \text{Item 21} + \text{Item 22} + \text{Item 23} + \text{Item 24} + \text{Item 25}} \times 100$$

or
$$\frac{\$1,086,000 + \$880,000 + \$120,700 + \$168,300}{\$16,459,000} \times 100$$

$$= \frac{\$2,255,000}{\$16,459,000} \times 100 = 13.70\%$$

Net Return on Invested Capital

Formula

$$\frac{\text{Net earnings (before extraordinary items)} + \text{total interest charges (after tax)}}{\text{Invested capital}} \times 100$$

Example

$$\frac{\text{Item 43} + (\text{Item 37} + \text{Item 38} - \text{both after tax})}{\text{Item 12} + \text{Item 16} + \text{Item 20} + \text{Item 21} + \text{Item 22} + \text{Item 23} + \text{Item 24} + \text{Item 25}} \times 100$$

or
$$\frac{\$1,086,000 + [(\$120,700 + \$168,300) \times .554^*]}{\$16,459,000} \times 100$$

$$= \frac{\$1,246,106}{\$16,459,000} \times 100 = 7.57\%$$

*Calculated as 1 minus apparent tax rate.
(See page 60 for calculation of apparent tax rate.)

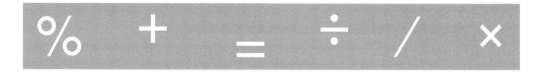

Net (After-Tax) Return on Common Equity

This ratio is comparable to the previous one since both ratios are calculated on an after-tax basis. This ratio is of prime importance to common shareholders since it reflects the profitability of their capital in the business.

Since taxes are an expense of doing business, the pre-tax return ratio has limited value as a comparison. Likewise, the net return on common equity does not provide a good comparison because the proportion of equity from capitalization to capitalization varies. Therefore, net return on invested capital can be the best overall measure of company-to-company performance.

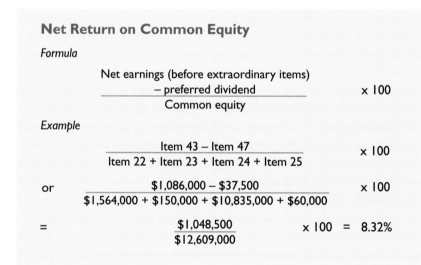

Net Return on Common Equity

Formula

$$\frac{\text{Net earnings (before extraordinary items)} - \text{preferred dividend}}{\text{Common equity}} \times 100$$

Example

$$\frac{\text{Item 43} - \text{Item 47}}{\text{Item 22} + \text{Item 23} + \text{Item 24} + \text{Item 25}} \times 100$$

or

$$\frac{\$1,086,000 - \$37,500}{\$1,564,000 + \$150,000 + \$10,835,000 + \$60,000} \times 100$$

$$= \frac{\$1,048,500}{\$12,609,000} \times 100 = 8.32\%$$

Inventory Turnover Ratio

This ratio measures the number of times a company's inventory is turned over in a year. It may also be expressed as a number of days, as shown in the example. A high turnover ratio is considered good. Also, from a working capital point of view, a company with

Analyzing Financial Statements

Inventory Turnover Ratio

Formula

$$\frac{\text{Cost of goods sold}}{\text{Inventory}} = \text{times}$$

Example

$$\frac{\text{Item 29}}{\text{Item 4}}$$

$$= \quad \frac{\$28,250,000}{\$9,035,000} \quad = \quad 3.13 \text{ times}$$

To calculate inventory turnover in days, divide 365 (days)
by the inventory turnover ratio:

$$\frac{365}{3.13} \quad = \quad 116.61 \text{ days}$$

To be most meaningful, the inventory turnover ratio should be calculated using cost of goods sold, as above. Since this information is not always shown separately, the net sales figure sometimes has to be used.

Formula

$$\frac{\text{Net sales}}{\text{Inventory}}$$

Example

As shown in the prior calculation, this ratio may be expressed in terms of the number of days required to sell current inventory, by dividing the ratio into 365 days.

$$\frac{\text{Item 28}}{\text{Item 4}} \quad = \quad 4.85 \text{ times}$$

$$= \quad \frac{\$43,800,000}{\$9,035,000}$$

or $\qquad \dfrac{365}{4.85} \quad = \quad 75.26 \text{ days}$

67

a high turnover requires a smaller investment in inventory than one producing the same sales with a low turnover.

This ratio indicates management's efficiency in turning over the company's inventory, which can be compared with other companies in the same field. It also suggests how adequate a company's inventory is for its business volume.

There is no standard yardstick for this ratio since inventory turnover rates vary from industry to industry. Companies in the food industry, for example, will turn over their inventory faster than heavy manufacturing companies, where a longer period of time is required to process, manufacture and sell the finished product.

If a company has an inventory turnover rate that's above average for its industry, it will generally mean that a better balance is being maintained between inventory and sales volume.

So there will be less risk of (1) being caught with a top-heavy inventory position in the event of a decline in the price of raw materials, or in the market demand for end products, and (2) wastage through materials and products standing unused for longer periods than anticipated with consequent possible deterioration in quality and/or marketability. On the other hand, if inventory turnover is too high compared to industry norms, problems could arise from shortages in inventory, resulting in lost sales.

Since much of a company's working capital is usually tied up in inventory, how the inventory position is managed has an important and direct effect on earnings.

Examples of high turnover industries: baking, cosmetics, dairy products, food chains, meat packing, industries dealing in perishable goods, and quick consumption, low cost item industries.

Examples of low turnover industries: aircraft manufacturers, distillers, fur goods, heavy machinery manufacturers, steel, and wineries.

VALUE RATIOS

R atios in this group – sometimes called market ratios – measure the stock market's rating on a company by relating the market price of its shares to certain figures obtained from its financial statements. The reason for this calculation is that price alone does not say a great deal unless there is a common way of relating it to dividends and earnings. Value ratios do this.

Percentage Dividend Payout Ratios

These ratios indicate the amount or percentage of the company's net earnings that are paid out to shareholders in the form of dividends. There are two kinds of payout ratios, namely, (a) on combined preferred and common dividends and (b) on common only. Note the different divisor in each case.

Percentage of Available Earnings Paid Out as Preferred and Common Dividends

$$\frac{\text{Total dividends (preferred + common)}}{\text{Net earnings (before extraordinary items)}} \times 100$$

$$\frac{\text{Item 47 + Item 48 in retained earnings statement}}{\text{Item 43 in statement of earnings}} \times 100$$

$$\text{or} \quad \frac{\$37,500 + \$350,000}{\$1,086,000} \times 100$$

$$= \quad \frac{\$387,500}{\$1,086,000} \times 100 = 35.68\%$$

Percentage of Available Earnings Paid Out as Common Dividends

$$\frac{\text{Dividend on common}}{\text{Net earnings (before extraordinary items)} - \text{preferred dividend}} \times 100$$

$$\frac{\text{Item 48}}{\text{Item 43} - \text{Item 47}} \times 100$$

or $$\frac{\$350,000}{\$1,086,000 - \$37,500} \times 100$$

= $$\frac{\$350,000}{\$1,048,500} \times 100 = 33.38\%$$

The dividend payout ratio indicates the percentage of earnings being paid out as dividends. Deducting this figure from 100 gives the earnings percentage remaining in the business to finance future operations. In our first example, 35.68% of available earnings were paid out as dividends in the year, so 64.32% was reinvested in the business.

An unstable payout ratio over the years usually means unstable earnings. Directors of some companies will try to maintain a steady dividend rate through good and poor times to preserve the credit rating and investment standing of the company's securities. If dividends are greater than earnings for the year, the payout ratio will exceed 100%. Dividends will then be taken from retained earnings. This would erode shareholders' equity.

Analyzing Financial Statements

Earnings per Common Share

Side by side with dividend per share, this ratio is one of the most widely used and understood of all ratios. It's easy to calculate and is reported commonly in the financial press.

Earnings per Common Share

Formula

$$\frac{\text{Net earnings (before extraordinary items)} - \text{preferred dividends}}{\text{Number of common shares outstanding}}$$

Example

$$\frac{\text{Item 43} - \text{Item 47}}{\text{Number of outstanding common shares per Item 22}}$$

or

$$\frac{\$1,086,000 - \$37,500}{\$350,000}$$

$$= \quad \frac{\$1,048,500}{\$350,000} \quad = \ \$3.00 \text{ per share}$$

Fully diluted earnings per share is a figure that's calculated on common stock outstanding, plus common stock equivalents such as convertible preferred stock, convertible debentures, stock options (under employee stock-option plans) and warrants, which enable the holder to become a common shareholder by converting or exchanging his or her securities. It shows the dilution in earnings per share that would occur if all equivalent securities were converted into common. Since Trans-Canada Retail Stores Ltd. has no convertible securities, assume Company ABC had the following:

• 1,000,000 shares of $2.50 Cumulative Convertible Preferred Shares, $25 par, that are convertible into common on a 1-for-1 basis;

• 2,800,000 common shares, no par value; and

• net earnings (before extraordinary items) of $10,455,000.

Earnings per common share using the formula above would be calculated thus:

$$\frac{\$10,455,000 - \$2,500,000}{\$2,800,000}$$

$$= \frac{\$7,955,000}{\$2,800,000} \quad = \quad \$2.84 \text{ per share}$$

Fully diluted earnings per common share would require the following adjustments:

• Since the preferred dividends would not have to be paid if the preferred were converted into common, the earnings available for the common would increase by the amount of the preferred dividends deducted, i.e. earnings would be $10,455,000.

• The number of common would increase by 1,000,000 since there are 1,000,000 preferred which would be converted on a 1-for-1 basis.

The formula is then:

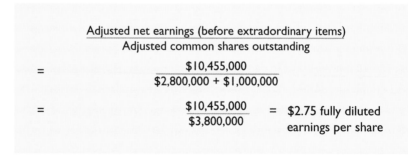

$$\frac{\text{Adjusted net earnings (before extraordinary items)}}{\text{Adjusted common shares outstanding}}$$

$$= \frac{\$10,455,000}{\$2,800,000 + \$1,000,000}$$

$$= \frac{\$10,455,000}{\$3,800,000} \quad = \quad \$2.75 \text{ fully diluted earnings per share}$$

Analyzing Financial Statements

In the case of a convertible debenture issue, an adjustment would have to be made to the interest, which would no longer have to be paid after conversion. This adjustment is necessary because interest charges are deducted before tax, and earnings are an after-tax figure.

For example, if the interest were $1,000,000 and the apparent tax rate of the company 40%, the applicable tax would be $400,000. So only $600,000 would be added back to adjust net earnings.

Because earnings from operations after all prior claims have been met belong to the common shareholders, they have a vital interest in knowing how much has been earned on their shares. If net earnings are high, directors may declare and pay out a good portion as dividends. Even in the case of growth companies, at least a token payment is often made because managements realize that most shareholders like to feel some profits are flowing into their pockets through dividend income. On the other hand, if net earnings are low or a loss has been suffered, no dividends may be forthcoming on the common.

Reducing net earnings to a per-common-share basis lets the shareholder see clearly how profitable his or her ownership interest in the company is, and whether dividends are likely to be paid. In the Trans Canada Retail example, net earnings are equal to $3 for each common share. Since regular dividends of $1 per share per year are being paid on common shares, the calculation also indicates that the dividend is well protected by earnings. In other words, earnings per common share are $2 more than regular dividend payments.

Since common share dividends are declared and paid at the company board of directors' discretion, no rules can be laid down to judge the amount likely to be paid out at a given level of earnings. Dividend policy varies from industry to industry and from company to company.

To estimate the dividend possibilities of a stock, the factors to consider include:

- The amount of net earnings for the current fiscal year
- Earnings stability over a period of years

- The amount of retained earnings and the rate of return on that
- The working capital position
- Policy of the board of directors
- Plans for expanding (or contracting) operations, government dividend restraints (if any)

Dividend Yield

Before a company is able to pay a dividend, it must have enough earnings and working capital. Then, it is up to the directors to consider the other aspects mentioned above and reach a decision on whether to pay a dividend, and to determine the size.

The yield on common and preferred stock is the indicated annual dividend rate expressed as a percentage of the stock's current market price. It represents the investor's percentage return on the investment at its prevailing market price.

Dividend yields allow for a superficial comparison between different companies' shares. What they don't show are differences in the

Dividend Yield

Formula

$$\frac{\text{Indicated annual dividend per share}}{\text{Current market price}} \times 100$$

Example

Assuming the current market prices of $49 for the preferred and $26.25 for the common shares of Trans-Canada Retail Stores, the yeilds are:

Preferred: $\dfrac{\$2.50}{\$49} \times 100 = 5.10\%$

Common: $\dfrac{\$1.00}{\$26.25} \times 100 = 3.81\%$

quality and record of each company's management, the proportion of earnings re-invested in each company, the proportion of preferred and common in each company's capitalization, the equity behind each share and, in the case of preferred shares, the difference in preferred dividend coverage. All these factors should be taken into account in addition to just comparing yield – preferably over several years. Only then can an informed evaluation be made and an investment decision reached.

Price-Earnings Ratio or PE Ratio

PE ratios are calculated only for common stocks and not for preferreds. The only relevance earnings have to most preferred shareholders is how well (or by what safety margin) they cover preferred dividends – and the "preferred dividend coverage ratio" measures this best.

The main reason for calculating earnings per common share – apart from indicating dividend protection – is to enable a comparison with the share's market price. The PE ratio expresses this comparison in one convenient figure. It's a short way of saying that a share is

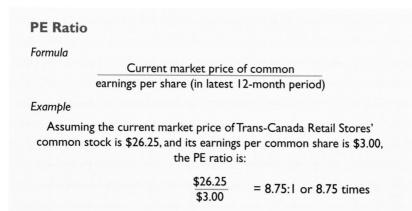

PE Ratio

Formula

$$\frac{\text{Current market price of common}}{\text{earnings per share (in latest 12-month period)}}$$

Example

Assuming the current market price of Trans-Canada Retail Stores' common stock is $26.25, and its earnings per common share is $3.00, the PE ratio is:

$$\frac{\$26.25}{\$3.00} = 8.75{:}1 \text{ or } 8.75 \text{ times}$$

selling at so many times its actual or anticipated annual earnings. PE ratios enable one share to be compared with another.

Example

Company A   – Earnings per share: $2; Price: $20

Company B   – Earnings per share: $1; Price: $10

Though earnings per share of Company A ($2) are twice those of Company B ($1), the shares of each company represent equivalent value because A's shares, at $20 each, cost twice as much as B's. In other words, both companies have a PE ratio of 10:1 (or are selling at 10 times earnings) – Company A, $20/$2; Company B, $10/$1.

PE ratios reflect the views of thousands of investors on the quality of an issue. The elements that determine the quality of an issue –and therefore are represented in the PE ratio – are:

• Tangible factors contained in financial data which can be expressed in ratios relating to liquidity, earnings trend, profitability, dividend payout and financial strength.

• Intangible factors such as quality of management, nature and prospects for the industry in which the issuing company operates, competitive position and individual prospects for the company. All these factors are taken into account when investors and speculators collectively (and subconsciously) decide what price a share is worth in terms of the number of times its earnings are expressed in its price.

To rate the PE ratio for one company's common with others, the companies must be comparable, which usually means they must be in the same industry. PE ratios for various industries are available from different sources, e.g. the TSE (Toronto Stock Exchange) Monthly Review shows PE ratios for 47 industry sub-groups of the TSE 300 Composite Index (see Table 3).

In the example, price-earnings ratios are calculated on a company's earnings in the latest fiscal year. In practice, however, most

Analyzing Financial Statements

Table 3

PE Ratios for Selected Industry Sub-Groups of TSE 300 Index – January 2000

	PE Ratio		PE Ratio
Banks & Trusts	10.01	Gas & Electric Utilities	11.53
Integrated Oils	25.06	Publishing & Printing	16.55
Department Stores	22.31	Biotech/Pharmaceuticals	68.28
Food Stores	11.73	TSE 300 Companies	34.11

Source: TSE Review, January 2000

investment analysts and firms make their own "projections" of a company's earnings for the next twelve-month period and calculate PE ratios on these projected figures in terms of the stock's current market price.

Obviously, with the variables and hazards involved in forecasting earnings, using "estimates" in calculations should be approached with great caution.

The PE ratio is probably the most useful and widely used financial ratio because it is, in fact, all the other ratios combined into one figure. It represents the ultimate evaluation of a company and its shares by the investing public.

Equity Value (or Book Value) per Preferred Share and Common Share

Preferred shares rank before the common in liquidation, winding-up, or distribution of assets. This is the preferred shareholders' legal right. When their prior claims have been met, the common

shareholders are entitled to share what's left.

The two ratios under this heading measure the asset coverage for each preferred and each common share.

Rules of Thumb for Equity Value per Preferred Share

• *Utilities* – Minimum equity value per preferred share in each of the last five fiscal years should be at least two times the dollar value of assets that each preferred share would be entitled to get if the company were liquidated.

• *Industrials* – Same as for utilities.

Equity Value per Preferred Share

$$\frac{\text{Preferred and common share capital + contributed surplus + retained earnings + foreign exchange adjustment}}{\text{Number of preferred shares outstanding}}$$

Example

$$\frac{\text{Item 21 + Item 22 + Item 23 + Item 24 + Item 25}}{\text{Number of preferred shares as per Item 21}}$$

or

$$\frac{\$750,000 + \$1,564,000 + \$150,000 + \$10,835,000 + \$60,000}{15,000 \text{ shares}}$$

$$\frac{\$13,359,000}{15,000 \text{ shares}} = \$890.60 \text{ per preferred share}$$

As the example shows, each preferred share is backed by $890.60 of equity in the company. Since the par value of the preferred is $50 (as stated in the balance sheet), the equity backing is $890.60 / $50, i.e. 17.81 times, well above the required minimum of two times. (If the preferred shares were redeemable at a premium on liquidation, the premium would be added to par value in the calculation in the previous sentence, slightly reducing the coverage, e.g. a premium of $2.50 on liquidation would result in equity backing of $890.60 / $52.50, i.e. 16.96 times.) As an added safeguard – besides meeting the minimum of at least two times liquidation value in each of the last five fiscal years – the equity value per preferred share should also show a stable or, preferably, a rising trend over the same period.

Equity Value per Common Share

$$\frac{\text{Common share capital + contributed surplus + retained earnings + foreign exchange adjustment (less preferred dividend arrears, if any)}}{\text{Number of common shares outstanding}}$$

Example

$$\frac{\text{Item 22 + Item 23 + Item 24 + Item 25}}{\text{Number of common shares outstanding as per Item 22}}$$

or

$$\frac{\$1,564,000 + \$150,000 + \$10,835,000 + \$60,000}{350,000 \text{ shares}}$$

$$\frac{\$12,609,000}{350,000 \text{ shares}} = \$36.03 \text{ per common share}$$

What constitutes an adequate level of equity value per common share? There's no simple answer. Although a per-share equity (or book) value figure is sometimes used in appraising common shares, in actual practice there may be very little relationship between the equity value per common share, and the market value per common share. Equity per share is only one of many factors to be considered in judging a stock. Many shares sell for considerably less than their equity value, while others sell far in excess of their equity value.

This difference between equity and market values is usually accounted for by the company's actual or potential earning power. A company with high earning power will command a better price for its shares in the market than a company with little or no earning power, even though the shares of both companies may have the same equity value. So no meaningful rule of thumb for an adequate book value per common share can be quoted.

OTHER SELECTED RATIOS

In addition to the ratios covered in this book, there are many others in common use. Some have a general application to most companies, e.g. price to equity per share ratio, working capital to stockholders' equity ratio, working capital turnover ratio (i.e. net sales divided by working capital), earnings per common share/dividend per common share ratio. Other ratios are used to analyze companies in specific industries, e.g. annual sales per square foot of retail floor area is a favorite ratio used to analyze retail chains such as food supermarkets.

In real estate investment, the cushion ratio is widely used. It measures in percentage terms net cash flow from a property relative to gross income. The banking industry also uses many ratios that reflect the special nature of its business. These include loan loss provisions as a percentage of loans outstanding and in cents per dollar of revenue.

It's possible to introduce new ratios that would cover almost every possible relationship. But the trick is not to increase but to limit the number of ratios, and get to know them so that you can interpret them in a meaningful way.

In this book we've calculated ratios for a single company for a single year. As stated earlier, one year's ratios alone do not tell you much. To be truly useful these ratios must be compared to competitors' ratios, to industry ratios, and from year-to-year for a period of five years or longer.

Now you have the information you need to look at a company's financial statements and see an accurate picture of its past and present performance.

Take that information – along with an idea of the company's future plans, an understanding of the industry in which the company operates, and of the economy in general – to help you make investment decisions that are right for you.

Index

Notes

Notes